IT ALL STARTS WITH
IMAGINATION

STANISLAVSKI AND ACTING

BY VICTORIA MAY

A Practical Guide to Acting

Based on Stanislavski's, "An Actor Prepares"

This is a Stanislavski-inspired training program based on the areas of actor development in "An Actor Prepares"

Published by
Scripts To Stage
www.scriptstostage.co.uk
© Victoria May

CONDITIONS OF SALE

All rights reserved. This publication is sold subject to the condition that it shall not, by way of trade or otherwise, be lent, re-sold, hired out, reproduced, in any form or by any means, mechanical, electronic such as information storage and retrieval systems, photocopying, manuscript, typesetting, recording or otherwise circulated without the copyright owners prior consent.

Victoria May has asserted her moral right to be identified as the author of this work.

A CIP catalogue for this book is available from the British Library.

ISBN: 978-1-912541-12-6

BookPrintingUK
Remus House
Coltsfoot Drive
Peterborough
PE2 9BF
Telephone: 01733 898102

All Rights Reserved
© Copyright 2018
ISBN: 978-1-912541-12-6

Printed and bound in the UK by BookPrintingUK
Website: www.bookprintinguk.com

PREFACE

Like many actors and directors, I navigated through all the key texts, looking for the wisdom and guidance needed to get closer to an ideal scene within my chosen art. I wanted to tell stories in the best and most authentic ways possible. I would read the masters of theatre acting, one after another—all slightly contradicting each other and all of them searching for similar things in very different ways. The theory books are one thing, but then putting them into practice is another thing entirely. The way to learn a practical craft is to put these ideas and theories into practice, or discover new ways to explain the phenomenon of the art of acting. I would always shy away from Stanislavski. I had very uncomfortable experiences in past workshops and felt most of the direction I experienced left me feeling slightly unsettled, out of the present and stuck in the emotions of the past.

So, I began to go through each text, line by line and really duplicate and understand the written ideas of Stanislavski and how he saw them manifest practically. I wanted to establish what he had intended, if that was being translated practically in actor training and illuminate and remove false application.

I have worked in schools throughout the UK and lectured in performing arts within the University curriculum, and each year I see students who arrive more and more confused about Stanislavski. I also witness a sadness and failure in students because they are unwilling to explore what some practitioners have been using, which is likened to a kind of psychoanalysis. It is damaging to artists and after extensive surveys, I find the confusions that come in between Stanislavski and the enthusiastic new student of acting are the areas to be addressed.

The workable practice that Stanislavski lays out needs to be put back in, with the spirit of play, enthusiasm and practical elements explored. This book attempts to create exercises that if explored with the above points in mind, then all participants should totally enjoy themselves whilst getting closer to their aim of being ever better at their craft.

I would also like to state that it is often thought that a group can explore a text and devise a text without reading it or using a dictionary to establish the words in the text and the nomenclature for that 'doctor' or 'era' or that 1600's soldier you are playing. It also has become apparent that there is vital necessity to work on a whole production when exploring Stanislavski. The majority of his guidance is based on that stable senior reality. For both these areas of concern, the problem of time comes to the forefront. But if a concise process is developed without cutting corners, fully realised characters, fully prepared actors and wonderful stories will be told. I've always been a dreamer, but most art and ideas start with the imagination. That's why the book is titled as such.

CONTENTS

Introduction   1

Chapter 1 Imagination   4

Chapter 2 Focus, Concentration & Interest   18

Chapter 3 Through the Body   28

Chapter 4 Units, Objectives & Actioning   34

Chapter 5 Playing Emotions   42

Chapter 6 Adaptation   48

Chapter 7 The Flow of a Role   52

Chapter 8 Communion   54

Chapter 9 The Super-Objective   58

Chapter 10 Full Production   60

References   62

INTRODUCTION

Born in Moscow Stanislavski witnessed the beginnings of the railway, automobiles, aeroplanes and the radio. He lived through three revolutions and WW1. Born into a golden era of theatre and performance arts, he had all the time in the world to establish a full exploration of all aspects of theatrical art and especially the art of acting. He had at his disposal all the splendour of a golden age. He did however transcend the political climates that inevitably opened up the theatre to all classes and a new era of actors who felt that life could be snatched away at any given moment. This forced him to change some of his deep-seated ideas.

When we explore Stanislavski's system, we are inevitably studying a master who has lived from the highest echelons of theatre splendour down to the base of what it is to make a true actor from the root and the very seed of artistic exploration.

He created a school. Not a school like the American or British drama schools of today. Although these schools teach Stanislavski, his school was very different. It had its acting students living on site, farming the land, building the sets, working and eating together. What was he trying to unearth? The core being of an artist! The essence of the human spirit is natively capable of full perception, emotions and imagination that a child manifests naturally. His aim: to rekindle these qualities and have the actor freely unleash them within the framework of the play, the performance and within the art of story telling.

The entire Moscow Art Theatre school enterprise aimed to *"bring together actors in good and interesting conditions in life, amidst healthy physical work, after the close and nervous atmosphere of the stage that always spoils peaceful relations."* (Stanislavski, (1924), 1974, p, 539).

When exploring this program of study, each student should keep a journal and have no fear of making mistakes or not achieving the outcome, but be able to reflect on the outcome and their mistakes. Within every exploration there is something to learn. Stanislavski's life in art is based on reflection, discovery—trial and error.

There are two main branches to his system. One branch pertains to the techniques that provide structure on stage and in every moment of performing. This includes analytically applied tools with script and how to read it as an actor. It also consists of how to apply diction, rhythm, tempo and what to do with the text and all the structural technical elements. However, there is the sentient side of the art of acting whereby the true artist achieves life in the character. This takes the student far beyond learning lines and avoiding bumping into the set.

This total exploration of the art of acting is the driving force behind Stanislavski. Each aspect of his system will be broken down and explored through practical exercises. Eventually the student will explore each separate aspect of his system, the sole aim being that all these aspects will then be happening simultaneously but with clarity and within the linear framework of the theatrical process...from page to stage. In "My Life In Art" Stanislavski states;

"Let the artist live, let him be enchanted, disappointed, happy: let him suffer, love and live through the entire gamut of human emotions, but let him at the same time learn to recreate his life and his emotions into art!" (Stanislavski, (1924), 1974, p, 38).

When we look at the chronological biography of Stanislavski we can see very early in his life in art he had to, through circumstance and the desire to get the play on, become the stage director.

Stanislavski's method is a systematic or step-by-step approach that works through each part of the process of realising and bringing to life a character. A series of exercises created for the student to concentrate the actor and react:

"... not only on his sight and hearing, but on all the rest of his senses. It embraces his mind, his will, his emotions, his body, his memory and his imagination. The entire physical and spiritual nature of the actor must be concentrated on what is going on in the soul of the person he plays" (Stanislavski, (1924), 1974,p, 465).

"When an actor is completely absorbed by some profoundly moving objective, so that he throws his whole being passionately into its execution, he reaches a state that we call inspiration" (Stanislavski, (1936), (1980), p, 310).

INTRODUCTION

Note: Stanislavski's "The Actor Prepares" was a one-year, full-time training course for his students. I recommend working through this training program in a linear order and ideally about three times through – then working on the final production.

CHAPTER 1
IMAGINATION

JUST BE TRUTHFUL! Have you ever said this or demanded it or been asked to demonstrate TRUTH?

What does Stanislavski mean when he talks about TRUTH? He is saying "truthful emotions." But how is this achieved? He means bodily and spiritually with full perceptions and creative urge. But how is this achieved? He states;

"The actor says to himself: All these properties, make-up, costumes, the scenery, the publicness of the performance, are lies. I know they are lies, I know I do not need any of them. But if they were true, then I would do this and this, and I would behave in this manner and this way towards this and that event" (Stanislavski, (1924), 1974, p466).

So to achieve 'truth' we have the 'as if'—the magical creative 'if'. To achieve magical creative 'as ifs' we use imagination. Like a child who invests in the world of play—the actual reality passes into an investment in a created reality. So what is needed?

- IMAGINATION
- PLAYFULNESS
- BELIEF
- TRUST

These four states should exist in the physical setting and the sentient emotion of the played out reality. You will know when you achieve this, as it feels fun, magical, freeing and TRUTHFUL.

When the student breaks down the elements of acting it becomes abstract and systematic, but the aim is for it eventually to all come together and become second nature.

When playing a role in a play, it is important to play the character from the character's perspective, driven by intuition and feelings. The character is within the world of the play. It is the audience that gets to see the complete picture. When preparing an analysis of the script as an actor, it is on a micro level or ground level that the character exists.

"Perhaps in our art there exists only one correct path—the line of the intuition of feelings! And out of it grow unconsciously the outer and inner images, their form, the idea and the technique of the role"(Stanislavski, (1924), 1974 p, 406).

The actor is concerned with the artistic actions, moment to moment from the beginning to the end of the play. How you prepare with the script will help create a strong foundation so you do not derail and start to view the play as the audience or the director does.

EXERCISE #1
INVEST IN THE REALITY OF DOING
(2 hour workshop based on "An Actor Prepares: ACTION")

Learning outcome: To feel the importance of a purpose on stage and to rid oneself of a general artificiality. This will be replaced with an investment in the reality of doing the action.

The result: Emotions will be produced as a consequence of the reality of doing an action with purpose and of course, the added barrier of a time constraint. The time constraint will raise the stakes and apply a bit of pressure. These constraints help the actor to stop thinking about the exercise and invest in the task set.

1. Split the group into two. One group observes and the other group participates in the exercise (observing is 50% of the learning process.)

2. Have half the group sit on the stage on chairs. Have them sit there for a length of time for no reason other than they are actors sat on a stage.

3. Discuss with the participants what this felt like.

4. Ask what the observing group witnessed.

5. Swap over the groups and repeat step 2.

6. Repeat 3 & 4 discussions.

7. Now with each group, give each actor the purpose within the time restraint of a 1 minute scene, to count all the ceiling tiles in the room or window panes – something difficult but not impossible to do within the allotted time.

8. Discuss the results with those performing the scenario and those observing. Compare the differences from when there had been no purpose to then having a purpose, within the added barrier of a time constraint. How did this feel different?

9. Now in groups of two, each actor is given a purpose and a task.

Example: Actor A has come to take actor B's bag away. Actor B knows that he/she has to give it to actor A but does not want to. The purpose for actor A is to take the bag and the purpose of actor B is to persuade actor A to change his/her mind. (An 'as if' can be created: Actor A is a teacher or parent or the original owner).

10. Give the student a few minutes to orient themselves with the task, any 'as ifs'–but not enough time to rehearse.

11. As a whole group, observe each group's improvisation. Explain to each group before starting that they will take 30 seconds of character B silently waiting. When improvising it is important to be in the room, in the moment and not thinking but simply being in the moment, whilst attempting to achieve your purpose. Explain that they have a time constraint of 1 minute per improvisation and put emphasis on whether the actor failed or is successful at getting his/her purpose fulfilled.

12. Discuss as a whole group what was discovered and how each actor felt and what it was like to observe. What occurred whilst 'waiting'? How necessary was it to speak? How invested were you? Where was your attention?

13. Move on to journal work.

14. Give each student the direct quotes from Stanislavski for their journal:

CHAPTER 1

"On the stage there cannot be, under any circumstances, action which is directed immediately at the arousing of feeling for it's own sake. When you are choosing some bit of action, leave feeling and spiritual content alone"(Stanislavski (1936), (1980), p, 41).

"On the stage it is necessary to act, either outwardly or inwardly" (Stanislavski (1936), (1980), p, 41).

"Given set of circumstances means the story of the play, its facts, events..."the conditions of the life of the characters, the production, the set, costumes—all the circumstances that are given to an actor to take into account as he creates his role" (Stanislavski (1936), (1980), p, 51).

Note: If you invest in the reality of doing the action, with purpose and within the given set of circumstances (a time constraint of 1 minute) then the right emotions for that moment will surface. Also what will occur is that the actor will be so invested in the task of counting, getting the bag or keeping it that they will move over from a state of trying to be interesting to a state of being interested in their purpose and the other character. The result of this cross over is a gap where the audience can then observe the actors freely and become interested in them and whether they achieve their aim or not. When an actor is fixed on being interesting it pushes the observer away, crowds the space and gives the audience no gap to participate in the scene.

15. Have each student write in their actor's journal what they discovered in each exercise, what they have realised, what they can improve on, what they observed and how this can be applied to the art of acting.

EXERCISE #2
THE MAGIC AS-IF
(2 hour workshop)

The Magic As-If can be used directly by the actor in order to connect with their character's mind set. For example, if your character has to rescue a child, you may have difficulty connecting with this experience. A possible solution is to put in place an as-if that is similar like – when you helped someone who was lost or injured or perhaps you had to keep calm whilst a friend was panicking. The main thing is to play with as-ifs till something fits. As-ifs are used on so many levels of creativity and assist imagination.

IT ALL STARTS WITH IMAGINATION

1. (The magic 'if' is a starting point in place of the given set of circumstances that a script offers.) Have the group seated facing the stage. Choose a participant, have them seated on the stage and ask them to go over and shut the door, or open it and then return to their seat.

2. Now have the participant create an, 'as if' with regards to the door which will add purpose. For example: there is a child sat behind it or a stranger who is crying. How would you open the door in that given set of circumstances?

3. Once the whole group have observed this then each find a partner for the next task.

4. Chose an action to explore. Each group of two will help each other to find an action each to carry out.

Examples:
- Opening the stage curtain.
- Clearing a table.
- Writing a letter.
- Tidying a room.
- Looking for a lost object.

Note: Keep it simple. Each participant within this structure uses their imagination to create 'as ifs'. Remind the participant that there is a moment of stillness and simply being there. In every moment on stage, action both internally or externally is happening. The groups of two should watch each other and ask each other questions to strengthen the 'as ifs'.

5. When the participants have explored this exercise for 20 minutes, bring the whole group together to observe each participant's exploration of 'as if' within the chosen scenario. After each one, see if the observers can clarify and understand what is occurring. Discuss and then move on to the next participant.

Note: "Remember for all time, that when you begin to study each role you should first gather all the materials that have any bearing on it, and then add to it more imagination, more 'as ifs' till you believe in what you are doing. In the beginning forget about feelings...feelings will come to the surface of their own accord" (Stanislavski (1936), (1980), p, 53).

EXERCISE #3
IT ALL STARTS WITH IMAGINATION
(2 hour workshop)

1. Form groups no smaller than 3 actors per group – a whole group extended improvisation is ideal.

2. Give each group a choice of setting and the notes from the suggested examples: 1, 2 or 3 (You may want to give each group a printed copy.)

   Example 1: You are in a pine forest, it has been snowing and it is 3am. Use chairs to mark out the forest.

   Note to students: Do not discuss this improvisation. Find a place. Take a few moments as individuals to sense the change in temperature...how tired are you? Allow your imagination to affect your body language and relationship with this environment. Allow your imagination to take over and let this lead into how you relate to each other. Take your time. Do not rush this or feel like you need to perform a scene. This is for you to allow imagination to find its way into the creative process.

   Example 2: You are in a town square, you have no money and it is an unknown town. It is 3am on a Saturday night. You have no phone.

   Note to students: Do not discuss this improvisation. Find a place. Take a few moments as individuals to sense the change in temperature...how tired are you? Allow your imagination to affect your body language and relationship with this environment, how you feel, and what emotions you experience. Allow your imagination to take over and let this lead into how you relate to each other if at all. Take your time. Do not rush this or feel like you need to perform a scene. This is for you to allow imagination to find its way into the creative process.

   Example 3: You are on raft, the raft has been at sea for three days and nights, it is battered and wind-swept and unstable. There are sharks in the sea. It is 3am. It is calm after a storm and the temperature is cool.

   Note to students: Do not discuss the improvisation. Find a place to be, within it. Take a few moments as individuals to sense the change in temperature...how tired are you?. Allow your imagination to affect your body language and relationship with this environment, how you feel, and what emotions you experience. Allow your imagination to take over and let this lead into how you relate to one another, if at all. Take your time. Do not rush this or feel like you need to perform a scene. This is for you to allow imagination to find its way into the creative process.

3. Once each group has positioned the chairs in the chosen improvisation, ask them to position themselves in the space. Take some time to sense the environment and the given set of circumstances and to imagine them. Start the improvisations. When they are in full flow observe each to see the transformations in body language, emotion and the limited dialogue that comes about through this exercise. What occurs is that the artist is finding that the process of imagination starts internally and then becomes manifest externally. Or in other words, the process of imagination starts spiritually, which then manifests in the physical universe. A much more truthful performance is created as each student is investing in 'as if' and the given set of circumstances.

4. After 30 minutes of extended improvisation, have each group sit together with their journals. Discuss what they found or discovered in this exercise, how they related to each other and what things they imagined individually and if this transcended to a 'shared group imagination' experience. Did they experience any barriers or freedom within this created world? How does this support the art of acting? Have them write their findings in their journals.

5. Ask each actor to write the following quote in their journal:

Stanislavski states, "Imagination creates things that can be or can happen, whereas fantasy invents things that are not in existence, which never have been or will be, but who knows, perhaps they will come to be." (Stanislavski (1936),(1980),p, 55).

Answer the following questions in your journal:

Stanislavski states, "On the stage there cannot be, under any circumstances, action which is directed immediately at the arousing of feeling for it's own sake. When you are choosing some bit of action, leave feeling and spiritual content alone"(Stanislavski (1936), (1980), p, 41).

Did you manage to achieve this today or did you add emotion before action? Write what you found happened for you, remember this is a learning process and you are reflecting.

CHAPTER 1

Stanislavski states, "On the stage it is necessary to act, either outwardly or inwardly" (Stanislavski (1936), (1980), p, 41).

"You may sit without a motion and at the same time be in full action" (Stanislavski (1936), (1980), p, 41).

Did you experience moments of inward and outward acting, or being still and yet experiencing full motion? Please write what you experienced.

How did this imagination exercise use what Stanislavski calls the given set of circumstances—the story of the play, its facts, events?

"the conditions of the life of the characters, the production, the set, costumes—all the circumstances that are given to an actor to take into account as he creates his role" (Stanislavski (1936), (1980), p, 51).

EXERCISE #4 Part A
IMAGINATION WITHIN THE GIVEN SET OF CIRCUMSTANCES
(2x2 hour workshop)

Does the playwright give a full description of the character in each play? No. It is the actor's job to read the script, understand all the words and definitions of words pertaining to the world of the script and to embrace the given set of circumstances—the story of the play, its facts and events.

"the conditions of the life of the characters, the production, the set, costumes – all the circumstances that are given to an actor to take into account as he creates his role" (Stanislavski (1936), (1980), p, 51).

But, within these circumstances—this form and structure—created by the playwright or devising team—there is a need for the actor to imagine (create things that can be or can happen) or use fantasy (invent things that are not in existence—yet). If a script states for example, 'he walks into the room', then the actor has to ask, but from where? From what? How? Why? And also, when? All these questions arise and if you are playing that character you MUST know the answer. You cannot play the scene in a general way. The audience will not believe you and it is more fun to have an intention in every action on stage.

Exercises that can help this begin with some initial script work. If you are playing a character in a play then it might injure the play if you forget the facts of that character and go into extreme fantasy. For example—I'm going to play Lady Macbeth as a horse that speaks in horse language. This would be leaving the initial text reading and taking it to a created reality. I exaggerate, but yet it might make for a brilliant take on that Shakespeare play. However if we are looking at the realistic, literal truth of a script then it is vital to have a close text reading of the characters, so each character works together with the others as the playwright intended.

Without reading the whole play its is impossible to fully identify your characters FACTS, PHYSICAL ACTIONS, INTENTIONS and PURPOSES in each moment and as the main OBJECTIVE within the story. However if one explores the facts of an opening sequence within a workshop exercise, then the actor has an opportunity to start to find the playwright's essence through the action—as a start point only. This exercise allows the actor to investigate the facts and the physical actions and play them out within a setting and with other characters. What starts to happen is that the actor's creative imagination connects with the physical actions, facts, setting and the other characters (the given set of circumstances). If we do this accurately and technically, then magically the character's basic motivation/ purpose/ super objectives start to present themselves. Answers start to arrive with regards to the key questions when playing a role: Where? What? How? Why? When?

> **Note:** Suggested scripts with just enough action described before the dialogue begins and for the purpose of this exercise (all taken from Gutenberg.org) are as follows:

"The Devils Discipline," by George Bernard Shaw. (2 female)

"The Master Builder," by Henrik Ibsen (2 males, 1 female)

"When We Dead Awaken," by Henrik Ibsen (1 male, 1 female)

"Six Characters In Search Of An Author," Luigi Pirandello (12 male or female)

1. Create groups with the required amount of characters.

2. Provide a copy of the opening scene for each group.

3. Have the groups read it through, clear up any definitions. Choose which character they will play (there is no dialogue, just action.)

4. Ask the actors to investigate very exactly and as accurately as possible the facts.

Example: It is 6pm, I am in a house. It is 1850.

5. Ask the actors to investigate what physical actions their character does from the beginning of the sequence to the end.

Example: I enter. I walk over to the window. I open it. I go to the oven. I remove a burnt pizza. I take it to the table. I sit. I stand. I leave.

6. It is vital for this exercise that the actors play the scene using only the facts and the physical actions they have identified so far.

7. Run the scene through with the facts and actions.

8. Discuss as a group how it felt, discuss what came up – any intuition and further understanding?

9. Investigate within your groups:
   - Where are you?
   - What are the facts?
   - What are the physical actions in sequence?
   - What season?
   - The time?
   - The space?
   - The form?
   - The country?
   - The political/social/economic climate?

10. Discuss/research/investigate together.

11. How do the characters feel towards each other in the scene?

12. Have the groups create the scenes based on their findings, and those findings only.

13. Discuss each character's basic motivation or main objective—based

on the actions and facts in the opening sequence and what you sensed when playing the scene.

14. Make a note in your journals of what you feel the basic objective is at this point in your work on the script.

15. Remember we are exploring the non-dialogue opening sequence of action to a whole play. Most of the answers will be in the play, which will inform one how to enter or exit. However it is often found in the playing of one scene that if you stay true to the facts and actions, then the true intentions arise and present themselves.

16. Rehearse the scenes once the group have an idea of their character's intentions. Add any as-ifs to carry out the basic actions.

17. Rehearse the scenes and present to the whole group.

18. Discuss together the facts found and the physical actions. Discuss how the preparation work supported the improvisation and if the organic creation (based on the facts) leads to a structured scene, which is similar each time it is run. Did a basic motivation arise for your character? How did this inform your as-ifs to enter and exit?

Note: Actors can consider the consequences of these facts and actions.

Example: The 'fact' a character hobbles in to the room and is tired all the time can be played many different ways. It is vital one gets all the data from the text one can before adding an 'as-if'. As-ifs are there as a prop to connect emotionally to an action, intention or scenario, but one's imagination is constantly creating now. So, in this example, my character hobbles...wow! How does she hobble? Let me see. The word hobble derived from Middle English and means to, rock from side to side. Do I know why my character rocks from side to side when walking? It says in the script she never had the right-sized shoes. Wow! This is a key fact! You see the facts start to paint the playwright's picture. You are a detective and you are also using imagination to develop the full, rich complete character in your own unique but accurate way. How they sit, eye contact, social status... the list is long when fully realising a character within a given set of circumstances. It is very important that each actor finds his or her own physicality. The true essence of the character will come from the life and livingness of each individual actor and the playwright's intentions. *"Let an actor remember that his own opinion is better than that of an outsider, better even than an excellent one, if only because another's opinion can only add to his thoughts without appealing to his emotions"* ("Creating A Role," Stanislavski, 1989,p, 5).

19. With the naivety of not knowing the rest of the play, true discovery of the character's essence can be found. However it is important to not make any concrete decisions until a full script analysis has taken place.

20. What are the limitations of this exercise? The actor needs to discover that to fully answer how to play this opening of the play, they will need to read the whole play individually to work out:

Who they are?
Why they are there?
How they feel about their position, their family, the setting...what it is like to live in this class and time?

What is the character hiding and how do they really feel? As Stanislavski states, *"to know is synonymous with to feel "*(Creating A Role, Stanislavski, 1989,p, 5).

Preparation for the next session:

Give each actor a copy of the full play.
Have them read the full play.
Clear all definitions in the text.
Make notes on the facts of their character and the actions.
Ask actors to work out what is the main overall objective/intention/motivation of their character for the whole play.

EXERCISE #4 Part B
IMAGINATION WITHIN THE GIVEN SET OF CIRCUMSTANCES
(A series of 2 hour workshop sessions)

Five 2 hour sessions forming one overall exercise:

1. (2 hr) Read the whole chosen play from Exercise #4 Part A with the same performance group. Understand all the words, the era of time and the playwright's work.

2. (2 hr) Group research of the era, the culture, the job or life relating to your character. (Scrapbook / images / notes, etc.) and really understand the world of the play.

- Look at your own life and who you know that may help relate to the character you will play.

3. (2 hr) Re-read (as a group) the play with all of the above research completed.

- Make notes in your journal on the facts of your character, the actions your character takes and if possible what is driving them throughout the play.

4. (2 hr) Give the groups 1 hour to rehearse the opening scene with no dialogue, straight into the full first scene with dialogue (for text with no scenes find an appropriate cut off point). Give notes before each group rehearses the scenes again.

5. (2 hr) Have the whole group rehearse, present and watch each group's scenes.

- Discuss as a whole group how reading the complete play informed the opening scene. Did your character's main objective change after reading and understanding the play as a whole? How did your physicality change or your attitude to the other characters?

- Make notes in your journal on comparing both experiences and also how the first exercise helped the second.

Note: Each 2hr session can be repeated and explored further. The group might spend two weeks investigating the world of the play for section 2.

EXERCISE #4 Part C
IMAGINATION WITHIN THE GIVEN SET OF CIRCUMSTANCES
(2 hour workshop)

1. With the characters played from Exercise #4, hot seat each character—paying special attention to their age, status and feelings towards other characters, the environment and their views of the world.

2. Go back to the opening scenes. Rehearse now with the script analysis and the hot seating experience and ask the actors to add any needed as-ifs that support the story telling.

3. Perform the scenes to the group.

4. Add the following quote to your journals

   Note: *"During every moment we are on the stage, during every moment of the development of the action of the play, we must be aware either of the external circumstances which surround us (the whole material setting of the production), or of an inner chain of circumstances which we ourselves have imagined in order to illustrate our parts".* From: *"An Actor Prepares"* (Stanislavski, (1936), (1980), p, 65).

CHAPTER 2
FOCUS, CONCENTRATION & INTEREST

EXERCISE #5
OBJECT OF YOUR ATTENTION
(1 hour workshop)

"You must have something which will interest you in the object of your attention and serve to set in motion your whole creative apparatus" (Stanislavski, (1936), (1980), P71).

1. Ask the group to select one object. Place it in the performance space.

2. Put your attention on that object.

3. Observe the item.

4. Ask, are you observing this object?

5. Let's see. Invest in the reality of observing the object.

6. If needed add an, 'as if'. A character in a play may have a certain connection to an object. You can build an imaginary set of circumstances with regards to this object if you like. Imagine that this object is a reminder of a chance you had, a lost love or a pleasurable moment. Use your imagination to connect and invest in this environment and that object you are looking at.

7. What do you notice about your chosen object? (Allow the actors to call out or ask themselves in order to invest in the reality of observing the object.)

8. How is your concentration?

9. Build a back-story?

10. Who are you in relationship to this object? Where did it come from and what does it means to you?

11. This will strengthen the truth of the task.

12. The enemy of this exercise according to Stanislavski is, 'MECHANICAL GAZING' (Stanislavski, (1936), (1980), P71).

13. Run this part of the exercise until each actor is invested and focused.

14. Ask the group to be seated and observe. Take it in turns to individually enter the space and observe the object.

15. Run a simple scene whereby each actor enters the space and sees the object, focuses their attention on it with their back-story, as-ifs and connection.

16. Keep the improvisation going for a good length of time to see if the actor can sustain that focus and concentration.

17. Discuss as a group what difference it makes to an audience member when the actor is totally focused and interested in something within the world of the play, as opposed to their attention being to a large degree on the audience.

18. Make notes in your journals on your chosen as-ifs and back-story. How does this exercise strengthen focus and concentration?

EXERCISE #6
ATTENTION AND INTENTION
(2 hour workshop)

The origin of the word, 'object' is Latin and means, 'for the thing put before the mind'. The concentration of attention on the object can now be explored in improvisations where there is also intention regarding the thing observed.

1. The following exercises give focus to an object and also require an intention toward it. Your role in the improvisation may be as a distraction to the character that is connected and focused on the object.

2. Select groups (example 3 is for actors working alone).

Example 1: A family reunion. One family member sees the only picture of him as a child and wants to take it to keep for himself. The rest of the family are about to announce that if he does not sort his life out in general, then he will be written out of his father's will. But he has to take this photograph.

Example 2: The grown-up children visit their father's house, which has been redecorated by his new wife, who hates them all. They are there on Christmas Day and on the fireplace is their beloved great-aunt's mirror, which they have been instructed to take. They have five minutes to establish a focus and attention on the object, what it means to each individually as well as how you intend to reclaim it.

Example 3: You are sat alone in your room. It is your last day before leaving home. Find an object that has significance, invest in this communication, depending on the object and the significance of it. How does this make you act? What do you decide to do?

3. Give the groups 20 minutes to rehearse these scenarios—fill the gaps in the scenario with a back-story and 'as-ifs'.

4. Perform them.

5. Discuss as a group each performance in relation to attention, intention, focus and concentration. Discuss how having barriers such as a 'fearsome father' or a 'yearning not to leave' can add to the scene.

EXERCISE #7
THE TABLE GAME
(2 hour workshop)

The purpose of this exercise is to observe and concentrate your attention on a character objective and to achieve the result of your objective. This is combined with focusing your attention on a physical object to extract as much detail as possible.

> **Note:** Somewhere in the middle of this exercise a connection, imagination and emotion will surface because of the sheer investment in objectives, action and purpose.

1. Have actors work in groups of 5 or 6 around the table.

2. Take it one group at a time to offer the observers the value of seeing the effect of this level of concentration whilst investing in trying to achieve one's objective.

3. A little role-play scenario begins, a group of friends sharing what they all did at work this week—the aim is to gain as much data about each other's lives as possible. There is 5 minutes to do so.

4. Before we start, choose an object to put your attention on.

5. Once the exercise begins, the director or educator will call out to increase the level of attention on the object (increasing on a scale of 1-10).

6. Put 2 out of 10 ratio of attention on your object, whilst trying to fulfil your character objective of gathering as much information as you can on what each person did in his or her job/studies/life this week. Check what was learnt and see who gathered the most... just for sport! When you call out the next amount, actors should add another degree of attention on to their physical object. Take it up to 10.

    Note: Regarding the chosen object: Notice its lines, form, colours, details, characteristics, what it reminds you of, what memories it conjures up in you, if you like it or to find something to like about it or value about it. Let your imagination create significances as well as you experiencing the conflict of fulfilling the character objective. Gather as much data as possible about these people to pass the 'test'.

7. Once the director/educator has reached 10 degrees of focus in approximately 5 minutes, discuss with the group what they found and how the character's objective and the increasing attention influenced their intention. Each actor will share what they found out from the other actors in the scene and what difficulties or success they had in regards to the struggle/battle/balance between attention and intention.

EXERCISE #8
SPHERE OF INFLUENCE
(2.5 hour workshop)

The circle of attention helps you focus your concentration on the area of action you are in and keeps you in the scene. The last thing you want to do is to have your attention pulled to something outside the world you are alluding to and trying to create in the act of story telling. Stanislavski in "An Actor Prepares" uses light to help the student understand and explore the circle of attention. Often students have not got access to stage lights, so to mark the space out we will use chairs, which serve a similar purpose.

1. Make a circle of chairs around a stage or area to perform in.

2. Separate to these chairs have the class outside of the stage area, observing from a distance.

3. Give each actor a few minutes to recall the individual table object from his or her previous 'table' exercise, as this should be very detailed.

4. Choose two participants to sit in the centre of the 'stage' with the circle of attention made up of chairs approximately two meters away from them.

5. The objective here is for one actor to use one of the following scenarios in relation to their chosen object.

   - Has found a suspected murder weapon.
   - A desired object one really wants.
   - A stolen item found and kept—a confession.

6. Actor A is playing the intention of any one of the above scenarios, whilst actor B reacts and develops an intention as the improvisation continues.

7. Allow imagination to enter in. The scenario is for the participants to have their attention in and up to the boundary of the circle of attention. Even though the circle of attention is marked out, you still have to imagine there is nothing beyond this circle. (Wherever possible, reduce the light beyond the circle of chairs).

8. Did the performers feel the circle of attention? Did they keep their focus within it and up to it?

9. Give all members of the group this experience, with a group discussion after each.

10. Move the group to a large hall, mark out the circle with a much larger outer circle.

11. Keep the same group of two but swap over the storyteller and the listener.

12. Give each group of two this experience.

13. Discuss as a group how this changed the performance.

14. Now in the same hall remove the chairs—select a couple of performers to run their scenario again but this time to imagine a small circle of attention in this large space.

15. Discuss as a group how this changed from when they first did the exercise with a larger and marked out circle of attention.

Note: For actor's journals, Stanislavski stated:

"As soon as your boarder begins to waver, you must withdraw quickly to a smaller circle which can be contained by your visual attention." (Stanislavski, (1936), (1980), P84).

EXERCISE #9
CREATING A CHARACTER- Observations and perceptions
(2.5 hour workshop)

1. Choose someone you know: a friend, a colleague, someone on your street.

2. Work in twos.

3. Take it in turns to describe your chosen person and help each other by asking lots of questions about this person—their habits, what they like or do not like, what they do on a daily basis, how

they react to the news, scandal, arguments—the more detailed the better.

4. Then individually find a space in the room and allow your imagination and understanding to explore this character mood. Move the character around the room, see how the character responds to tasks, objects...sense the stillness of the character. You will create your characters both physically and in attitude. Allow the character to react to a concentration of attention.

5. Once you find the character and have explored him/her for about half an hour, ask students to come out of character. Now make notes of what they found in terms of their change in physicality and attitudes. Look at how your imagination helps, what objects became significant to the character, how the circle of attention helped or perhaps was not relevant at this stage of developing a character.

6. Team up with your original partner and take it in turns to go into character whilst the other partner asks you questions in character for 10 minutes, then swap over. Always ask your partner to come out of character.

7. Have a discussion as a whole group on what you have discovered here.

8. Choose a scenario:

   - A community group meeting regarding the state of litter in the neighbourhood.

   - A hospital waiting room.

   - An interview for a job.

   - A traffic accident with observers giving their statement.

9. Have groups of various numbers with their newly developed characters improvise within the scenario. Let this improvisation run with the actors staying true to the attitudes, opinions and physicality of their newly developed characters.

10. Run the improvisation to explore character and character

interactions but for this exercise leave objectives alone—let the motivations of your character be discovered.

Note: Invest in the reality of doing but also listen and sense the character for it to surprise you with his/her true intentions. Often in extended improvisations, the answers to what the basic fire of the character is arrive rather than making concrete choices to begin with. Making concrete choices too early may block a much more complex character development from surfacing.

EXERCISE #10
DETECT FALSEHOOD
(1 hour workshop)

STANISLAVSKI TALKS ABOUT FALSEHOOD. *"When you point out to him the palpable absurdity of some false action he has taken he is more than willing to cut it"* (Stanislavski, (1936), (1980), P131).

1. Create a scenario whereby the actors are searching for something. Place a wallet or purse in a hiding place before they enter the space.

2. Have the participants look for it.

3. As the actors are searching you can call out:

    - Are you investing in the reality of finding this object?
    - Are you being interesting for the audience now?
    - Or are you so interested in your task that the audience can enjoy watching you carry it out without any interference?

    Note: Build the comments up—almost to a point that you become a distraction.

4. Stop the exercise and state,

"the nagging critic can drive an actor mad and reduce him to a state of helplessness…search for falsehood only as far as it helps you to find truth. Don't forget that the carping critic can create more *falsehood on the stage than anyone else, because the actor whom he is criticising involuntarily ceases to pursue his right course and exaggerates truth itself to the point of it becoming false. What you should develop is sane, calm, wise, and understanding critic, who is the artist's friend. He will not nag you over trifles, but will have his eye on the substance of the work"* (Stanislavski, (1936), (1980), P133).

5. Now set the task up again—this time with another lost item. Be kind in tone and keep it playful. Encourage the actors to push through any barriers to their full investment in the reality or action. A time limit put on the task builds the necessity and investment in the task.

6. Ask these three questions sporadically throughout the task:

    - Are you investing in the reality of finding this object?

    - Are you being interesting for the audience now?

    - Or are you so interested in your task that the audience can enjoy watching you carry it out without any interference?

NOTES

CHAPTER 3
THROUGH THIS BODY

EXERCISE #11
GENERAL WARM-UP
(30 minute workshop)

1. Find a space.

2. Stand with legs shoulder width apart and in your own time visualise and bend vertebra by vertebra down for 24 parts before coming up for the same amount.

3. With instrumental classical music playing (eyes closed) have the whole group move each of their muscles to the music in their own space.

   Note: We are not looking for beautiful dancing but a warm up that allows each actor to explore each muscle in their own body and to stretch and extend and relax them.

EXERCISE #12
RELAXATION OF THE MUSCLES
(30 minute workshop)

So as not to be tense in the high moments of a character's journey, the key thing to find is the balance between tense moments and relaxed moments. The actor needs to control the body to remove tenseness when it happens during the action of playing a role.

1. In an empty space, have all the students lay on their backs on the floor.

2. Ask each student to identify the tense parts of their body and ask them to visualise relaxing them—giving up the contraction and resistance—allowing that part of them to sink into the floor.

3. Work through all the areas of tenseness with the aim of having the whole body relax into the floor with no resistance.

4. Certain muscles, in the action of playing a role, need to resist and contract to move and support other movements and actions. This is an opportunity to relax all those muscles. Relax them to a passive state and remove any unneeded and habitual tensions that have become stuck.

EXERCISE #13
THE CENTRE OF GRAVITY
(30 minute workshop)

1. In groups of five, have one person in the centre of the circle whilst the other members of the group provide a supportive wall.

2. With eyes closed and following the relaxation of muscles exercise, have the central participant rocked by the circle—gently and in slightly different directions. Have the central actor sense the shift in muscles relaxed and muscles tense and establish a freely adjusting process of moving between a tense then relaxed state of play.

3. Take it in turns till all actors have explored this phenomenon and feel that they can do this freely and flexibly and sense that it is 'mind over matter'.

EXERCISE #14
POSE AND IMAGINATION
(2 hour workshop)

1. Have each actor find a space.

2. Think of an every day activity—playing with shifts in his/her centre of gravity—complete one unit of movement based on that task. You could be calving a cow; making a bed...the list is endless.

3. Invest in the full physical exploration of this task. Create approximately 5 units of motion. Exaggerate each move, identify where the muscles are tense or relaxed (it is surprising how making a cup of tea uses leg muscles).

4. Now add resistance. Tense your muscles and try to stop yourself carrying out the task—exploring this resistance until you feel that the mimed out actions are using the full body and have resistance and definition. Remember to exaggerate these units and actions. Imagine the weight of the 'blanket', 'kettle' or 'rope'. With imagination and life experience you can estimate the amount of resistance and identify which muscles are required.

5. After exploring the actions/mime in an exaggerated fashion, bring it to a more internal and condensed version—still be aware of the tensions.

6. Rehearse the task now whilst describing what you did yesterday evening.

7. Watch some of these 'scenes' together as a whole group. Now bring three or four actors together in the same setting. Ask them to improvise their actions whilst talking to each other about their evening. (Those that have created movement tasks that relate to each other should be put together to help the setting and narrative).

EXERCISE #15 Part A
CHOOSE AN ANIMAL
(2 hour workshop)

1. Each actor should choose a character they have particularly wanted to play.

2. What animal well suits your chosen character's temperament and attitude to life? What are the actions and intentions of that character, for example is the character like a hunter? Is the character you have chosen timid or easily scared? Really take your time to revisit your chosen character, the playwright's description of them, the plot, their actions and objectives.

3. Once you have chosen your animal, start to study it.

4. Watch wildlife clips, look at books and artist's impressions.

5. Make notes on where their centre of gravity is during their daily

actions, how they hold their body and where the muscles contract and relax.

6. Explore the balance between physicality, text and opposition—between getting the physical task done whilst having the intent to communicate what you did last evening. Write up your findings and add pictures to your journal.

EXERCISE #15 Part B
EXPLORING YOUR CHOSEN ANIMAL
(3.5 hour workshop)

1. Whole group to complete warm-ups #11, 12 & 13.

2. All students should explore the full animal physicality in a shared space in the room for approximately 30 minutes.

3. When you can see the students have fully invested in the reality of doing this and are transformed physically, introduce gradient stages of metamorphosis into their chosen human character.

4. They are in the character of full animal, call out 9, (explain to the students before beginning the exercise that the scale of 10-1 will represent the transformation of full animal to full character). The aim is to have the animal fully existing but underlying the fully established human character.

5. Work through the scale—but don't rush—allow each stage to be fully realised and what will be discovered is that each actor will find the right ratio of animal/character balance for the character to fully communicate to the audience. This is before words even enter into the scene.

6. Once the exercise is complete have the actors identify their personal ratio of animal/character. Ask them to make notes in their journal.

7. Each actor will then choose a small monologue from their chosen script and prepare a small entrance (non-verbal), a small scene (verbal) and then a justified exit. The monologue is adjusted to

suit the needs of this exercise, which is to establish the animal/character ratio with the group/audience observing.

8. Prepare the monologue in terms of the character facts, actions, attention, intentions, as ifs and the physical actions along with this added animal characterisation work.

9. Rehearse over 3 workshops (always start with the full group warm ups #11, 12 & 13)

10. Have a sharing of each participant's 5-minute scene and subsequently their exploration into animal work and the tension/relaxation/control of body and muscles. Look at how the actor's imagination can control and affect the character's voice and mannerisms.

NOTES

CHAPTER 4
UNITS, OBJECTIVES & ACTIONING

EXERCISE #16
BREAKING THE SCRIPT UP
(2 hour workshop)

UNITS AND OBJECTIVES (6 x 2hr workshops or a play in a week project)

It is important to state that in using units and objectives, they are solely there for the preparation of a role. These tools are to help break down and fully realise sections of the text, but inevitably you will arrive back at the play as a whole. It is also important to identify what a unit is and that too many units would confuse the actor. Units are a tool and should be workable for the sole aim of achieving the whole part in the play.

When dissecting and analysing a play, Stanislavski states:

"Do not break up a play more than is necessary, do not use details to guide you. Create a channel outlined by larger divisions, which have been thoroughly worked out and filled down to the last detail." (Stanislavski, (1936), (1980), P115).

So how do we do this?

1. Choose a full text to work on for the whole group. Give each actor a copy of the text.

2. Distribute the parts.

3. Ask actors to spend a week reading the text, clearing up any words in a dictionary, researching the landscape, referenced places and things, the era of time and make notes on the script as a whole.

4. Each actor will identify the facts of the play and their character, the actions, their intentions and basic fire or motivations—their character's objective as a whole.

5. Read the play as a group (All actors must have a part—two or three plays may be explored in smaller groups if needed).

6. The first question is: What is the core of the play?

Stanislavski states that this is: *"The thing without which it cannot exist?"(Stanislavski, (1936), (1980), P116).*

7. Discuss this as a whole group and identify, 'What is the thing without which the play can not exist?'

8. Once a clearly defined and simple but dominant answer is established with a strong degree of certainty, go over the main points of the play without going into too much detail. (It is often helpful to write this out on large sheets—especially as the units can change as the group becomes clearer and more confident with the text).

9. The main UNITS are all the parts of the play essential to achieving the main established message or core. In Macbeth for example, the play cannot exist without introducing the character of Lady Macbeth or the Sergeant's account of "brave Macbeth" in battle in Act 1, Scene 1(Shakespeare, 1984, 1.2)

10. Now let's look from the beginning to the end of our play and see what main points are essential—these will be noted on the paper. These are the organic or naturally unfolding events that make the whole. When you have a huge scene such as Act 1, Scene 3 in Macbeth it is helpful to break the scene up into units of action—especially for both Macbeth and Banquo as they enter into an established scene with the witches, and talk with them. The witches vanish, leaving both characters alone before both Ross and Angus enter into Macbeth and Banquo's existing action. They leave and we are left with Macbeth having an aside or soliloquy and finally Banquo and Macbeth alone again before they head off to see King Duncan. A quick scan through this scene and six units seems to feel right in breaking up the scene—only to provide sections to analyse and understand more closely—they will eventually flow into one scene again and this is solely to help the rehearsal process.

11. Now identify the main super/whole play objective for your character as well as your scene objectives or objectives for each

UNIT of action.

12. These will shift and change, but essentially they will provide a start point to understanding the scenes and play.

13. Work through the text together with the director/educator, guiding the process till you all have a workable script, broken down into units and objectives.

14. Have the actors write in their journals their findings and the helpfulness of units/objectives.

Note: Breaking the script up into units and objectives does not have to be a slow and cumbersome and theoretical activity. Once you have read the play through you can work together to get a rough sketch of units and objectives—just enough to get it on its feet and in manageable sections. Here is a quick and brisk example using Macbeth—just enough to get it on its feet! Remember units and creative objectives can change, just like the action verbs behind the delivery of you lines. It might just be a way into what can seem like a sea of words at first.

Macbeth Example:
In Macbeth, there are strong messages of corrupt power, unchecked ambition, kingship and tyranny, hallucinations, mysticism, witchcraft, prophecy and the supernatural. There is also the *pathetic fallacy of the weather dominating the witches' opening scene and reflecting and strengthening the atmosphere of prophecy and supernatural events throughout the whole play. But what is the thing without which it (the play) cannot exist?

*A literary devise. The assignment of human emotions to non-human aspects of nature, which in turn can reflect the mood of the charcter's and overall atmosphere.

A: Objective Of The Play:
For me, it is ambition in both Macbeth and Lady Macbeth and the consequences of removing all in their way in order for him to become and stay king. The supernatural atmosphere is also a dominant factor:

- "All hail, Macbeth! That shalt be King hereafter" (Shakespeare, 1984, 1.3:50). Banquo states, "and great prediction of noble having, and of royal hope...speak then to me, who neither beg, nor fear, your favours nor your hate." (Shakespeare, 1984, 1.3:60-61).
- Banquo is not ambitious and identifies Macbeth as, "rapt with-

al" (Shakespeare, 1984, 1.3:57).
- Despite the witches' prediction to Banquo, *"Thou shalt get kings, though thou be none"* (Shakespeare, 1984, 1.3:67) Banquo warned Macbeth,

> *"But'tis strange:*
> *And oftentimes, to win us to our harm;*
> *Win us with honest trifles, to betray's*
> *In deepest consequence"*
> *(Shakespeare, 1984, 1.3:124-126).*

This foreshadowing by Banquo indicates to the audience that there will be consequences for meddling with supernatural powers but unlike Banquo, Macbeth chooses to give it life—based on his desires and ambition to be King. The journey to tyranny in order to fulfil those desires, now implanted as a prophecy by the witches, plays out the tragedy of Macbeth.

B: Some Circumstances Surrounding The World Of Macbeth:
There are supernatural meddlings by witches and sprits in amongst the desires and ambitions of Macbeth and Lady Macbeth.

- The witches cause harm to those they wish to trouble.
- There is a battle in which Macbeth shows great courage.
- There is a prophecy relayed to Macbeth and Banquo.
- Macbeth meets King Duncan.
- King Duncan is a good man.
- Banquo was Macbeth's dear friend.
- Banquo represents loyalty and honour and is faithful till his death.
- Lady Macbeth is ambitious and active in the supernatural world.
- When Macbeth weakens, Lady Macbeth overtly and covertly manipulates him and holds him accountable to his earlier promise.

Note: Continue throughout the play to get a general first 'brainstorm' of the 'essential parts' and become familiar with the key parts.

C: Medium & Smaller Units In Macbeth Includes:
For Example in Macbeths opening scene, Act 1, scene 1 you could break it up into 3 units:

Unit 1
Pathetic fallacy—atmosphere and mood established—weather/setting/mood.
(Creative Objective - to set the mood & atmosphere)

Unit 2
Entrance of the fateful witches - the Weird Sisters ('wyrd' or 'weird' derives from 'fate') In the original myth, Clotho, Lachesis and Atropos worked together with regards to human fate, determining the individual's death. This unit establishes the witches' power over the play as well as creating confusion and chaos.

- The prediction of foul air—foul play.

- The witches contradict themselves, which sets up the difference between reality and illusion—this also creates an unhinged, unpredictable atmosphere.

- The words they speak which Macbeth later speaks as his own words, which gives the reveal that the witches are working mysticism and witchcraft on and through him.

(Creative Objective: The all-knowing witches set the time to meet Macbeth so that this supernatural meddling will commence)

Unit 3
They Exit
(Creative Objective: mystery and supernatural communion)

> **Note:** The breaking down of this particular scene or any section of a play is for one reason and ONE PURPOSE:

- "At the heart of every unit lies a creative objective" (Stanislavski, (1936), (1980), P116).

Shakespeare also sets up the witches as a force here that allows the reader some sympathy later for Macbeth—they work on his desires.

- "When the battle's lost and won"(Shakespeare, 1984, 1.1:4).

They already know the outcome. This should be recognised as significant in how it is played and with what intention because it allows the audience to question: How in control is Macbeth of his own destiny? This is a very important frame of mind for the audience, as we still need to care for him in some measure.

But be aware;

"The mistake most actors make is that they think about the result instead of about the action that must prepare it." (Stanislavski, (1936), (1980), P, 117).

And remember:

Units and objectives are tools to create a *"logical and coherent stream"* (Stanislavski, (1936), (1980), P, 117).

So with this in mind, at the heart of every unit lies a creative objective. The intention of the line can also be the unit. If you are playing a witch and the creative objective is to establish when you will all meet Macbeth, then the actions played out will also communicate to the audience that he has no say. You predict what will happen and it does. The message this gives dominates the whole play. You just have to play your actions, your intentions, your creative objective within the setting and atmosphere—which is your character's native environment. These all add up to the given set of circumstances.

We can now also add the intended effect of the line spoken. What are you doing with that line? What effect are you trying to create? In the case of Witch 3, there is a 'confirming'—"I confirm." But also there is scope for the actor to take a beat and get that knowledge from the sky or cauldron or storm and therefore it is that which feeds the witches' ability to confirm:

- *"There to meet with Macbeth"* (Shakespeare, 1984, 1.1:8).

There are so many ways to communicate these creative objectives throughout a play.

The physical and spiritual nature of man is intertwined so often in action and motion. What you do physically is directly related to a manifestation of what is going on spiritually.

D: The Character Of Macbeth:
The super objective of Macbeth could be said to be becoming King.

"The objective always has a verb" (Stanislavski, (1936), (1980), P, 123).

You could extend this to; 'to fulfil his ambition of becoming king'. In your objective you must have some action. If you are playing Macbeth, it could be further developed into: 'I wish to remove all in the way of me becoming the King'.

But he has objectives for each scene or unit. Here are some examples:

- I wish for a sign.
- I wish for my ambitions to become reality.
- I wish to overcome this first hurdle.

Note: There are plays that have no scenes, just acts. Units can allow the actor a gradient approach to the play and attack the script in bite size units at first. Ultimately units and objectives are tools to help the actor and director to confront smaller parts of a larger journey, resulting in a richer and more complex playing of the role. There is also the process of Actioning the text. It is a form of scoring the lines with appropriate transitive verbs. Choosing an action verb can help get closer to expressing the chosen intention and motivation for each line.

EXERCISE #17
ACTIONING YOUR SCENE
(1-1.5 hour workshop)

1. Take one of the scenes you are working on.

2. Have the whole group seated in a large circle around the action.

3. Whilst the actors are performing the scene, ask the group to call out action verbs that might seem appropriate or challenging to play the lines with.

4. This demands the actors keep focused and not distracted whilst applying the action verb called out.

5. As a director/educator control the pace that the action verb runs for and how many are called out. (This exercise is playful and often it produces humorous versions of the scene. It can also unstick fixed ideas of how a line ought to be delivered and allow a less serious, more playful approach which in turn may produce the truthful essence of a line of text).

6. Allow all actors in the play to experience this process.

7. Write your findings in your journal and any discoveries on how a line might be delivered (this of course can and often does change).

8. If you decide actioning is effective, then ask each actor to action his or her characters text throughout the whole play. The play can then be rehearsed with the continuation of these techniques if required. You can shift and change the action verbs in order to get closer to the essence and purpose of the play.

CHAPTER 5
PLAYING EMOTIONS

Our own emotions and life experiences can connect with the characters we play. It is widely misunderstood that we should experience the full emotional memory that we choose to match with the character's events. This false idea of emotional memory would in fact take us away from the moment and would become destructive to the truth of the moment on stage. Moreover, "These direct, powerful and vivid emotions do not make their appearance on the stage in the way you think" (Stanislavski, (1936), (1980), p, 175).

An actor who understands his character, the play and is fully invested in the actions—living the part—will inevitably connect and a channel is left open which will arouse feelings. It is always YOU playing that part. Your own feelings and connections will become analogous with that of the character. To achieve this, exercises which connect the actor with the material, whilst leaving a channel between the character and self will bring about an emotionally connected performance.

Done incorrectly, you end up with the actor mentally absent from the stage, stuck in some past event which weakens the artist and often violates the truth of the character. Re-living his own emotions and often experiencing them again produces a painful experience for the artist but also, often a damaging experience. Actors are valuable and creative. Exercises need to be understood around the area of emotions. The key is to be courageous, connected and let the emotions surprise you, as the best acting moments are in the moment and unique. But then the next moment is there and so the actor needs to be fully in the command seat as a professional to be true to the next moment and tell the story. If they are caught up in some painful past memory then what actually happens is that painful event steals the experience from the audience and repels them.

Often it is very contrary emotions that surface in life and on stage in the given circumstances—it would be a mistake to try match emotion with a stock event, for example hearing that a loved one has died and then recalling grief memory. This would result in repelling the audience and take the actor out of the present. The key is to just be open and let go, trusting that connections will be made.

EXERCISE #18
EMOTIONS IN STORY TELLING
(3 hour workshop)

1. In pairs, take it in turns to tell each other a story that happened in your life that had an emotional impact on your life. A story the actor is comfortable talking about. The purpose of telling the story is so the pair can then take their partner's story and make it their own.

2. When telling your story make sure to give as much detail on a sensory level: what you could see, smell, hear, feel, touch...the mood and atmosphere and emotions.

3. Start at the end of the story, working back to the beginning of it— then retell from the beginning to the end. This way you will identify the unbroken line and the changes in objectives along the way.

4. Spend 20 minutes sharing each other's stories in this way and allowing your partner to ask questions about the setting/circumstances and any further details.

5. Now in your pair, take it in turns to make your partner's story your own. It is important to stay as closely to the original as possible with attention to all the details (this is the equivalent of having a first hand discussion with the playwright).

6. Practice with each other for an allocated time.

7. Each group of two take a seat on the stage or in the space whilst the rest of the group observe. Watch each actor perform their story to their partner.

8. As observers; look and be open to the inner force of the mind, intellect and feelings in action.

9. Discuss how connected or unconnected these characters and their story are.

10. Now each actor should close their eyes and visualise the image of the event, change it from past tense to present tense and only speak the words as you imagine and visualise the mock up of the event. Tell the story in the present.

11. Now as a whole, watch each actor deliver the story in this way.

12. Discuss as a group from observing and participating HOW these directions change the level of connection with the story.

13. The result is that there is a channel opened from the artist to the material with a more authentic and emotionally alive performance.

EXERCISE #19
EMOTIONS IN MUSIC AND MOTION
(1 hour workshop)

- Choose a variety of music from various genres.
- Create a large circle with a space in the centre.
- Play the music and have each actor take their turn in the centre —eyes closed to connect with the music and dance.

1. Those on the outside must observe the central dancer and allow mimicry to take place. True investment leads to a closer, more truthful essence of expression.

2. Allow plenty of time for each participant in the centre, so as to let any falsity fall away. True connections happen—firstly with the lead dancer then with the group. A deeper connection emotionally is achieved on many levels—with oneself, with the whole group and for the artist to tune up their sense of sound, motion, listening, feeling, rhythm and overall kinaesthetic awareness.

3. This exercise can often be used as a warm up, with the music and influences pertaining to the play you are working on. The result is a more in tune emotional/sensory connection using music to have a work-out. This leads to an openness to the material, the character you are playing and the whole world of the play.

EXERCISE #20
OBSERVING EMOTIONS
(2 hour workshop)

To achieve a connection to the character you are playing, you build up an identity with the facts, habits and consequences of that character's life.

As an artist you will connect, have empathy and with imagination a transformation does take place whilst you are still you. This is unique every time and emotions will vary, as long as the artist remains open and committed to their character.

In order to achieve this detailed connection with a character, the following exercise is created to fine tune the skills needed.

1. Ask the group to go to a busy area such as train station or market square.

2. Choose a person in that environment to observe.

3. Independently observe the chosen persons mannerisms, mood, physical characteristics, interests, how they communicate to others, their habits, emotional tones expressed and also the overall tone the person levels off at between the moments of change.

4. Bring these observations back to the workshop space.

5. Make a large circle with a chair in the centre.

6. Take it in turns to 'hot seat' the observed characters.

7. The director/educator should ask the actor to go into character and after the exercise to come out of character.

8. The director/educator can interject and ask the actor to exaggerate the details to awaken the character and add a strengthened commitment to the reality of being this new individual. A transformation may not occur fully at this stage—this is an exercise to show how detailed one's study of character should go—in preparation for a transformation to occur.

IT ALL STARTS WITH IMAGINATION

9. Now ask the group to think of someone that they know well in life.

10. Put the actors in groups of two.

11. Ask the groups to take it in turns to ask detailed questions about each other's chosen characters. Explore the characters in front of each other.

12. Ask each actor now to find a space in the room of their own choosing.

13. Ask them to go into character.

14. Ask them to explore the surroundings and each other in character. This should be an extended improvisation that is no shorter than 30 minutes. This will allow the actor to fully indulge in the reality of this character's behaviour.

15. Ask the actors to emotionally connect with the character and use imagination to establish how they respond to others and the environment. Imagination and playfulness is key here, as it will lead to something more authentic.

16. Play music in the background—how does your character respond?

17. Staying in character, create short scenarios:

    - Family dinner
    - A waiting room
    - A party.

    Choose a selection of characters to improvise the scenarios. Add details or added information like 'they all have a secret and each needs to find out what each other's is'. This will add structure to the scenario. Go straight into improvising the scenarios without rehearsal.

18. Always ask actors to come out of character at the end of the exercise.

19. Discuss the findings as a whole group in terms of empathy towards the character and the choices the character made separate to what the actor would. Make notes in relation to how emotions entered into this charcter work.

NOTES

CHAPTER 6
ADAPTATION: COMMUNICATING IN THE MOMENT CONTRARY TO LOGIC

When playing characters, often we play people who are not logical or in charge of their emotions. Often when observing human beings you witness contradiction, irrational moments juxtaposed with moments of joy and rational thought. The actor who is present on stage, who knows what the character's objectives are can adapt themselves to the ever-changing circumstances. Often the emotional reactions that occur are contradictory, impulsive and reactive to other characters in the moment. This is courageous acting, alive and different but still true for each performance. The actor is able to react to each moment knowingly and remain in control — playful with the game of adapting. Adaptations can be absurdly contradictory but is part of human nature.

In "My Life in Art" there is a description of how a mother receives the news of the death of her son. In the very first moments she expresses nothing but began hurriedly to dress. Then she rushed to the street door and cried, "Help!" (Stanislavski, (1936), (1980), p, 233).

This adaptation or adjustment was spontaneous and with vivid feelings. This is an example of unexpected opposition within the given circumstances. It is rare that a person actually has the ability to totally confront what news or events are presented — often people take a while to comprehend life events. Survival is the driving force behind it all and in this example 'to dress' is the non-confront survival thing to do for this individual. Playing characters demands that the actor understand these human characteristics in the business of presenting characters in stories for an audience.

EXERCISE #21
ADAPTATION: IDENTIFYING INTERNAL CONTRADITIONS
(30 minute workshop)

1. Find a space in the room, sit down peacefully and remain silent for 5 minutes. Your objective is to 'sit peacefully' and 'empty of any thoughts'.

2. After this time, discuss with the group where the mind wandered to and what they thought about.

3. Ask, did this have anything to do with the task in hand (to sit down peacefully and remain silent for 5 minutes)?

4. This is to show the fact that each individual has contradictory and often absurd contradictions happening internally and externally at any given time.

5. Watch a few examples as a group and instruct the actor to invest in the objective but also to allow the adaptation.

EXERCISE #22
PLAYING WITH ADAPTATION
(2 hour workshop)

1. Give out chosen duologue scenes for groups of two to work with. (Preferably with a heightened emotional reveal within the scene).

2. Take time to face each other, read the lines out (clearing up any definitions).

3. Decide together each character's facts, actions and objective.

4. Rehearse the scene.

5. Allow yourself to note any spontaneous adaptations or opposing reactions you can use.

6. Make a note of these in the rehearsal process.

7. When performing the duologues to the group, run them with the note to keep playing, allowing the adaptations to occur and reacting to the other character in the moment. Discuss what they found and ask the group if they could identify what each character's objective was and any curious reactions, contrary to 'logic'.

8. Run them a second time, but this time with some improvised additional factors to challenge the choices made.

9. Select a few of the scenes to observe as a clear demonstration of communicating in the moment contrary to logic.

NOTES

CHAPTER 7
THE FLOW OF A ROLE

The unbroken line is a flow or a journey that is one whole journey. This is driven by the fundamental objective of that character within the story. This continuous whole is achieved later in the process after the dissecting of scenes, rehearsal, mimicry, developing and realising your character. It is a wonderful feeling to realise your journey as that character from the beginning of the play until its end. The following exercises start with short lines of action which progress into one continuous journey with its ups and downs/peaks and troughs. The aim is to feel that unbroken line or journey and know its worth.

EXERCISE #23
THE UNBROKEN LINE IN MOVEMENT
(30 minute-1 hour workshop)

1. In pairs, create a physical action/reaction sequence of movements (full body) based on love and hate and roughly 4 moves each.

2. Repeat till the moves are remembered.

3. Remove the pairing and with imagination repeat moves 1-4 without your partner's body.

4. Now work on making each move flow into the next—reaching move 4 and allowing that to flow to move 1.

5. Rehearse whilst adding the original intentions and objectives and sensations.

6. Take it in turns to present this dance or unbroken line of movement.

7. This will lead to the exercise regarding an unbroken line in text.

EXERCISE #24
THE UNBROKEN LINE IN TEXT
(2 hour workshop x3)

1. In pairs, tell each other what you did yesterday starting with the end of the day working back, e.g. I slept, before that I turned all the lights off, before that I wrote a list of what I planned to do the following day etc... make sure they are fixed in your memory.

2. Once the participant has worked backwards, they will then work forwards. The episodes will be clearly defined units that build up a whole line of events.

3. Once you both have a line of unbroken action, take it in turns to add what you did up until the present time and what will happen after the workshop, into the evening.

4. You will both have an unbroken line that flows from past to present to future.

5. Together explore the changing objectives, feelings, thoughts and sensations.

6. Now still in your pair, choose a known Shakespeare character you can both work on together.

7. Starting at the end of the play, take it in turns to map the unbroken line of events from the end to the beginning. Then start from the beginning to the end. Make notes, discuss and really invest in mapping the character's journey out.

8. Identify the various objectives (section by section) for your chosen character. Make notes.

9. Prepare one small monologue of your chosen character each. Direct each other making sure to allow the unbroken line to play out and see if the feelings, thoughts and sensations surface.

CHAPTER 8
COMMUNION – COMMUNICATION BEYOND WORDS

Communion is the sharing of thoughts and feelings—mentally and spiritually as artists working together in the art of performing characters and the level of connection and communion from character to character.

Both the dancing exercise (Exercise#19, Emotions in Music and Motion) and the retelling of your partner's stories with eyes closed (Exercise #18 Emotions in Story Telling) allow the possibility of tuning up the skill of communion.

EXERCISE #25
SPIRITUAL AND PHYSICAL CONNECTIONS
(2 hour workshop)

1. All actors memorise a monologue from a play they have fully read (10 lines max, distributed to each participant).

2. The learning of the text can be achieved in the session within groups of two. Each participant (after choosing one from a play they have already read) will recite a line to their partner who then repeats it back until both have memorised approx. 10 lines of text.

3. This preparation stage is actually a communion, which can be discussed once the exercise is complete. If a true communion had taken place and the percentage of listening and communicating was balanced, then more than likely, each person will have learnt 2 monologues—not one.

4. Each actor now performs to their partner—a living object—to which the character's feelings and actions are directed on the stage (you can also use an inanimate object). The object of the character's attention has to have significance in the form of an 'as-if' or back-story.

5. When performing, have a sense of the audience on a spiritual communion level—a very light invitation to feel.

6. Whilst the group observe, have each actor perform their monologue in *"direct communication with that object on stage, and indirect communication with the audience"* (Stanislavski, (1936), (1980), p, 208).

7. Discuss together what was observed after each participant's performance. This will help each actor who performs next. Allow the comments to affect the next actor's understanding of the exercise.

8. Once complete move on to each monologue delivered as, *"self-communion"* (Stanislavski, (1936), (1980), p, 208) with no object (person or thing which the feelings and actions of the character are directed at). Just choose a selected few to demonstrate the intensity this self-communion adds to the monologue. Ask the actor to come out of character.

9. As a group, discuss what was observed after each participant and allow the comments to affect the next actor's understanding of the exercise.

10. Once complete, move on to communication with an absent person or thing or imaginary person or thing (Stanislavski, (1936), (1980), p, 208). For example: Hermione in The Winters Tale having a private communion with her 'dead' daughter that she still senses as very alive.

11. Discuss as a group what was observed after each participant and allow the comments to affect the next actor's understanding of the exercise.

EXERCISE #26
CONTROLLING SPIRITUAL AND PHYSICAL COMMUNICATIONS IN CHARACTER WORK
(2 hour workshop)

1. The group sit on chairs in a large circle. Each actor takes it in turns to be seated in the centre.

2. When in the centre your objective is to communicate what you did yesterday to educate the audience—the storyteller will provide

a full sensory and detailed description, which may have long silences and pauses to recall such details.

3. Once started the group will take it in turns to call out a new action verb – give at least a minute for each to be explored.

4. As a member of the audience:

    - Do you get a sense of communion?
    - Do you sense and receive the story-teller's given intentions?

5. Does the participant in the centre invest in the reality of transmitting this intention?

6. Make notes of any observations in your journals.

NOTES

CHAPTER 9
THE SUPER-OBJECTIVE

The super-objective is the big WHY. It is the purpose for the character's existence in the world of the play. There are objectives to be achieved in each scene. These scene-by-scene objectives (achieved or failed) are all motivated by the super-objective. The best way to fully explore the super-objective is to look at a whole play. This is because there are three fundamental requirements in Stanislavski's system that all other aspects of acting the role hinge upon. The best way to analyse the super-objective is to compare what others find in the same material.

EXERCISE #27
THE BIG WHY
(1 day workshop or 3x2hr workshops)

1. As a whole group, read a full play out loud, clearing the definitions only. Choose a play with 4 or 5 characters and which has a beginning, middle and end. As a whole group understand: the text, the story, the setting and any specific terms pertaining to that world.

2. Once this step has been achieved then break the whole group into groups of 4 or 5 (one participant per character).

3. Now as a group choose who is taking responsibility for which character.

4. Discuss in your groups what the super-objective is of each character. On huge sheets of paper sketch out the through line of action, the facts and the given set of circumstances for each character.

Example: Work out–

- What are the character's through line of actions? (Work out the character's physical actions throughout the play— what does he/she do?)

- Write a list of the given circumstances:
  Who are you?
  Where did you come from?
  What room is this?
  Who does it belong to?

- Make a list of the facts of the character.

- Break the through line of action into units or sections that have their own objective (whether achieved or not). The objectives in each unit are emotional actions (use transitive verbs).

- What is your chosen character's super-objective?

5. As a group, present your findings to the rest of the workshop group, explaining what each character's objectives are per unit and what drives them and what is their super-objective. As a director/educator check some of the FACTS found about characters and the action line.

- See how this compares with each group's findings from the same play and characters.

- After a comparison of the findings, you should be very close and often have similarities regarding the super-objective. Use the group discussion to further the decision of each character.

CHAPTER 10
FULL PRODUCTION

In "An Actor Prepares," Stanislavski in the voice of the student states, *"I am comfortable, I know what to do, I have a purpose in being there, I have faith in my actions and believe in my right to be on the stage"* (Stanislavski, (1936), (1980), p, 280). In the context of this paragraph the student was feeling disappointed with the system. He goes on to discuss wanting to be 'inspired'. This is a vital point. To be inspired comes from the livingness of the artist themselves. What a privilege to have a codified approach to the role so that one can then move more freely in the role. The artist can then be free within this system to allow natural creative inspirations and emotions and impulses to manifest.

EXERCISE #27
FINAL PRODUCTION
(3 Week Production)

Choose a play whereby all the group have a character—only one character per person. Or choose a variety of plays for smaller casts in order that each actor has one role to fully work on. The purpose of the final production is to put in to practice all the theory/practice so far explored into a final production. It is very important to prepare and perform the whole play.

The process will begin with:

1. Casting the play.

2. Have each actor work privately on the text by reading it through lightly and clearing any words and concepts. Note what are the facts of your character and what actions do you carry out from the beginning to the end of the story.

3. Having a read through as a whole group.

4. Discussing the super-objective of each character—not deciding as yet.

5. Breaking the play down into units and each character's objectives or action verbs for each scene.

6. Clean up any facts chosen that are actually adaptions or lies as you work through the text. Work on the given circumstances of the character – What room or place they are in? Who surrounds them? What brings them here? (Work as a group and outside of workshop time to research the era and the world of the play).

7. Hot seating the characters on facts alone.

8. Decide the line of action and re-look at the super-objectives.

9. Read through again making adjustments and discuss further.

10. Get it on its feet—working on blocking each unit of action. Allow the actors to explore their imagination and 'as ifs'. Use the circle of attention and concentrations to play the objectives. Allow the actor to give birth to the emotional journey as it arrives. What are you doing with that line? What effect are you trying to create in the other character and why?

11. Move through the process of rehearsals, interjecting with any exercises from this training pack to strengthen the actor's preparation.

12. Once the play is constructed and the characters are fully realised then a sharing of this production takes place.

13. The student then will reflect on how they applied each aspect of 'IT ALL STARTS WITH IMAGINATION'. They should reflect on all aspects of the process and attempt to identify how they felt about their character and this process.

"It is necessary for the actor to develop to the highest degree his imagination, a childlike naïveté and trustfulness, an artistic sensitivity to truth and to the truthful in his soul and body. All these qualities help him to transform a coarse scenic lie into the most delicate truth of his relation to the life imagined" (Stanislavski, (1924), 1974, p, 466-467)

REFERENCE LIST

Konstantin Sergeevich Stanislavski, My Life in Art, Routledge (1974), ISBN 0-87830-550-5 (hardcover). University Press of the Pacific (2004) ISBN 1-4102-1692-6 (paperback).

Stanislavski, K, An Actor Prepares (Eyre Methuen Drama Books) (Performance Books) Published by Methuen Drama, 1980 ISBN 10: 0413461904 / ISBN 13: 9780413461902

http://www.gutenberg.org

Heartbreak House George Bernard Shaw, http://www.gutenberg.org/files/3543/3543-h/3543-h.htm

The Devils Discipline, by George Bernard Shaw. http://www.gutenberg.org/files/3638/3638-h/3638-h.htm

The Master Builder, by Henrik Ibsen, http://www.gutenberg.org/files/4070/4070-h/4070-h.htm

When We Dead Awaken, by Henrik Ibsen http://www.gutenberg.org/files/4782/4782-h/4782-h.htm

Six Characters in Search of an Author, Luigi Pirandello http://www.gutenberg.org/files/42148/42148-h/42148-h.htm

W, Shakespeare. (1984). Macbeth. Edited by Kenneth Muir. London: Methuen. 1.1:10

W, Shakespeare. (1984). Macbeth. Edited by Kenneth Muir. London: Methuen. 1.3:50-127